THE PARENTS' GUIDE TO BABY SIGNS

*Early Communication
with Your Infant*

Leann Sebrey

Illustrated by Valerie Nelson-Metlay

GALLAUDET UNIVERSITY PRESS
Washington, DC

Gallaudet University Press
Washington, DC 20002
http://gupress.gallaudet.edu

Printed in the United States of America

Library of Congress Cataloging-in-Publication Data

Sebrey, Leann.
The parents' guide to baby signs : early communication with your
infant / Leann Sebrey ; illustrated by Valerie Nelson-Metlay.
p. cm.
Includes bibliographical references.
ISBN 978-1-56368-398-5 (alk. paper)
1. Nonverbal communication in infants.   2. Interpersonal communication
in infants.   3. Infants—Language.   4. American Sign Language.
5. Sign Language—Study and teaching (Early childhood)
6. Sign language acquisition.   I. Title.
BF720.C65S43 2008
419′.1—dc22
2008045052

THE PARENTS' GUIDE TO
BABY SIGNS

CONTENTS

PREFACE

Self-expression is taking on new meaning in regard to infants, toddlers, and preverbal children (children who do not yet express language). Using American Sign Language with this group of youngsters, whether they are deaf or hearing, will promote a new recognition of their cognitive abilities as well as give them the ability to share with us their specific interests and desires. In my experience, infants as young as four months of age can learn to express preferences, needs, and desires.

Any time communication improves, frustration tends to decrease and the bonds and respect between individuals have the opportunity to strengthen and grow. These are also the benefits we see from using sign language with preverbal hearing children. Early communication is one of the very best things for your baby to experience. When signing is used with young children in daycare and classroom environments, the noise level decreases, learning becomes more productive, and children have fewer violent outbursts.[1]

I wrote this book primarily for parents, family members, caregivers, and educators of preverbal hearing children. However, hearing parents of deaf children will also find it useful. In these pages, we will explore American Sign Language skills and techniques and perspectives on teaching signs to preverbal

Young toddler signing
PLEASE

Toddler signing
CELEBRATE

children. You will also find tips for successfully applying your new skills to home, daycare, and classroom environments. My fondest desire is that you find the process rewarding and that the young people in your life will be positively affected.

We stand at the edge of a new age in the parenting, caregiving, and teaching of infants and toddlers. With American Sign Language, we can offer beneficial experiences to very young preverbal children. The children and families of our communities deserve this enriching and empowering opportunity. For our children's sake, let's get the sign out!

ACKNOWLEDGMENTS

I thank my loving husband Patrick, who is my strong anchor and my trimmed sails all at the right time. Patrick took the photographs in this book and, as you will see, he has an uncanny ability to snap the perfect shots of our babies using sign (which is no easy task). Thank you, Patrick. I also extend my heart in appreciation to our children—Adam, Melanie, Sean, and Aleah; without their understanding and willingness to support me in yet another project, this book would still be unfinished. My brother Greg, who came to this world without hearing, has taught me how to appreciate life—visually, audibly, and kinesthetically—and the importance of sharing that appreciation with others. Nancy Darlington, mother of dear Jessica and Nyssa, is a close friend and a gifted teacher. She is also a champion for educating caregivers; her very presence emanates optimism and respect for all children. Alison Ames, the mother of a neat young lady named Veronica, is very talented at design and formatting. Alison has been essential in taking my ideas and developing them into a book. Karen Colburn Wilbanks, who is fluent in five languages, is a friend and the mother of an awesome young man named Colburn. Karen, who has added ASL to her repertoire, graciously took on the task of editing my work. We have the best friends in the world; thank you all.

It is also very appropriate that I acknowledge the pioneers in the journey of bringing sign language to hearing infants and toddlers. The deaf community has shared the beautiful gift of American Sign Language with the hearing families of the world. I want to thank the parents, caregivers, and early childhood educators who took a leap of faith in the exploration of using sign with hearing babies. A special thanks to the researchers whose work gave evidence to what we now refer to as fact: Douglas Abrams, Catherine Brown, Marilyn Daniels, Kimberly Weatherly, Carolyn Rovee-Collier, Jana Iverson, Olga Capirci, Maria Cristina Caselli, Joseph Garcia, David Hammer, Philip and Elizabeth Prinz, Linda Acredolo, Susan Goodwin, Brie Moore, Sharon Gretz, Adele Abrahamsen, Nicola Grove, Virginia Volterra, Stephen M. Edelson, Yvonne Emmons, Chris Boyatzis, Ronnie Wilbur, Brenda Zinober, Margaret Martlew, Susan Goldin-Meadow, Heidi Feldman, Laura Namy, and Sandra Waxman.

May we all be blessed with love, a sense of peace, and the insight to appreciate the power and wisdom of children. Thank you, babies!

INTRODUCTION

Have you ever wondered what your baby is thinking? Research shows that signing babies actually speak earlier, have larger vocabularies, and show increased self-esteem indicating higher IQ (Intelligence Quotient) and most likely EQ (Emotional Intelligence) as well.[2] Infants who use signs can communicate their thoughts, needs, and ideas. What a tremendous gift to have a window into your baby's thoughts and to be able to respond with less frustration! I have experienced this as a pediatric nurse, a teacher, and as a mother. When our youngest son learned the sign for *flower* at 10 months of age, he immediately began sharing with us his interest and love for horticulture. Every plant, flowering or not, was inspected, identified, and appreciated. By teaching that one sign, we gave Sean a way to tell us what he found interesting and what caught his attention. His gentleness and curiosity toward flowers was able to grow, and now we have a greater understanding of the unique interests of our little boy. He is also my number one gardening assistant, and we both love every minute we spend together in the garden.

Experience and research is now demonstrating that parents and caregivers who are willing to learn and use a few

An ASL Class for child development therapists

basic American Sign Language (ASL) signs can facilitate more effective communication with their preverbal hearing children (see the selected references at the end of the book). Many ASL signs are iconic; in other words, the signs actually mimic the actions or behaviors that they represent. Therefore, the signs not only make sense, they also instinctively can become a very natural method of communication.

I have signed for many years. My younger brother has a significant hearing loss, and he received his first set of hearing aids when he was three years old. I was almost nine when my parents arranged for my first signing class, and ASL has been an integral part of our family life since that time. My four wonderful children all sign to varying degrees. With our youngest, I used the only sign that a breast-feeding newborn has any interest in, NURSE!* Our toddler can sign absolutely

---

*Words in capital letters represent signs.

anything he is shown, and he uses the signs very appropriately. He also readily speaks using basic sentence structure. Our older children sign as needed to communicate with their uncle and the babies. A sign we find ourselves frequently using, one that will survive in our family for generations, is I LOVE YOU.

With signs, we can communicate across a crowded gymnasium or through the windows of an airport. If you are searching for the very best thing you can do for your baby, start with good communication. It is an essential component in building and maintaining trusted, healthy, and loving relationships.

As a proponent of using ASL with hearing infants and toddlers, I speak and teach nationally, working to raise awareness of the benefits of signing with young children. This book is the result of hard work, years of experience and research, and the cultivation of the tools I use to teach parents, caregivers, and educators every day. Over the years I have taught thousands of adults how to sign with babies. I discuss scientific research as a foundation for using sign with preverbal hearing children, practical techniques for learning sign language (even as a novice), and the fundamentals of growth and development. I include child- and family-oriented signs, providing the necessary tools for parents of young children to be successful. Hearing babies who sign tend to speak earlier, have more self-esteem, and experience much less frustration than nonsigning babies.[3]

This book is designed to provide the tools that parents, caregivers, and educators need to be able to sign with very young hearing children. These techniques will provide the building blocks for two-way communication months, if not years, earlier than usually anticipated. I realize that parenting young children leaves little time or energy for intense, uninterrupted study time. I commend all of you who are seeking the best things for your child. Your baby and your family will be forever enriched.

1

Laying the Foundation for Using American Sign Language with Babies

Children naturally gravitate to movement and gestures. Any combination of voice, verse, music, and movement is usually irresistible for youngsters. Games such as peekaboo and songs like "If You're Happy and You Know It" captivate young children. Babies participate gleefully in "Itsy Bitsy Spider" well before they develop the vocal skills to sing. In fact, one of the first documented studies on the use of signs by hearing babies began when Linda Acredolo noticed that her infant daughter created and used gestures to convey her needs. Acredolo and Susan Goodwyn, with funding from the National Institute of Child Health and Human Development, conducted a ten-year study (1989–1999) comparing the use of signs, verbal cuing, and other typically used communication patterns with young hearing children.

All of the children participating in this study were in their first year of life when it began. The parents of babies in group 1 were taught symbolic gestures for frequently used items or activities. The parents of the infants in group 2 were instructed to use strong verbal cuing or to sound out words when speaking with their child. The parents of infants in group 3, which was the control group, were given no

| A one-year-old signing MORE | Preschooler signing STOP |

special instructions about how to communicate with their children.

Acredolo and Goodwyn found that, by the age of two, the signing children had an average of 50 more words in their spoken vocabulary than the nonsigning groups of children. By the age of three, the children who signed as babies actually had the language skills expected of four year olds. Acredolo and Goodwyn assessed all the children again in second grade and found that youngsters who signed as babies (group 1) had mean IQ scores that were 12 points higher than the children who did not sign (groups 2 and 3).[4]

Dr. Marilyn Daniels of Penn State University compared Peabody Picture Vocabulary Test scores of pre-kindergarten children who signed as babies to those who did not sign. The results of this study are also remarkable. Daniels found that children who signed during their preverbal stage scored significantly higher (meaning they had larger vocabularies) than those who did not sign.[5]

In 1999, Dr. Kimberlee Whaley of Ohio State University conducted a study in the campus childcare center. Her results indicate that signing in childcare settings significantly reduces noise levels and decreases the frustration levels of staff (and, most likely, children too). Caregivers are then able to spend more time in nurturing interactions with the children rather than in crisis management. The need for conflict resolution is significantly reduced as well.[6]

Joseph Garcia also promotes the use of signs with hearing preverbal youngsters, but unlike Acredolo and Goodwyn and others, he advocates the use of ASL signs. Garcia monitored babies who were exposed to ASL and concluded that the use of established signs rather than homemade gestures was incredibly beneficial to the babies' language development. His technique is well documented in the *SIGN with Your BABY* publications.[7]

American Sign Language is the preferred language of the American Deaf community. It is also useful for those hearing individuals who have little or no spoken language abilities. ASL has been used successfully with children who have apraxia, autism, Down syndrome, and learning and reading disabilities. In addition, inclusive and multilingual classrooms that incorporate signs for all children find communication barriers can be markedly reduced.[8] As a nurse I have found that patients big and small will readily use signs to communicate their thoughts and needs in certain medical situations. Signs like PAIN, MEDICINE, TOILET, YES, NO,

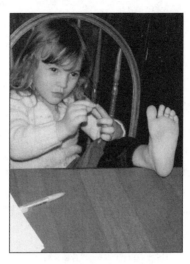

Toddler signing
HURT/PAIN

EAT, and DOCTOR can be easily taught to post-operative patients, as well as patients who require mechanical ventilation or are receiving certain other therapies.

Acquiring Language

Current research supports the theory that infants have the cognitive ability to receive and understand language much earlier than ever before expected. The timeline for developing expressive language is different between signing babies and those who rely only on oral communication. From birth to about six months of age, most babies cry and coo to express themselves. Around six months, babies begin to babble, that is they produce what seem to be random sounds. By 12 to 15 months, they can produce one-word utterances that are identifiable words from the parents' language. A child typically can be expected to begin using simple two-word phrases at one to two years of age. Telegraphic (more concise) speech, using relatively full sentences, and the learning of appropriate tenses and word order can be expected to begin at three to four years of age. Most children acquire two-thirds of their everyday vocabulary by their third birthday.[9]

In contrast, typically developing infants who are exposed to and learn ASL can develop the ability to express themselves well before their first birthday.[10] Sean at one year of age had a vocabulary of more than 100 signs, and by 18 months his verbal aptitude matched his signing proficiency. Aleah could sign her basic needs when she was four months old. Our children's knack for signing may seem extraordinary, but these are typical experiences for families who commit to using ASL signs.

2

Why Use ASL with Hearing Children?

As I said earlier, American Sign Language (ASL) is the primary language of the American Deaf community. ASL is a complex, visual/gestural language that incorporates handshapes, large and small movements in different directions, eye contact, facial expressions, body posturing, pantomime, space, and context to convey meaning. Many of the handshapes come from the manual alphabet (see p. 66). ASL is not a visual form of English; its grammatical structure is significantly different from English. Young children relate to the expressiveness and energy of ASL. The old saying "actions speak louder than words" definitely holds true with ASL. While signs are the basic vocabulary of ASL, the emotion and energy associated with a sign convey important information about the exact meaning of the sign. For example, the sign for *cold* is made by clenching the fists and shaking the body as if you are shivering. Young children remember this action when they encounter something cold, like an ice cube or snow.

Young signing children will use a single sign to convey an entire sentence, just as beginning talkers use one word to communicate a complete idea. For example, after finishing her cereal, a signing baby may sign MORE to tell you she

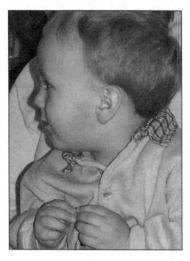

Toddler signing MORE

wants more to eat. This is the same meaning that is conveyed when a toddler says "more" after finishing her cereal.

So why use American Sign Language with hearing infants and toddlers rather than random, homemade gestures? First, because ASL is the third most frequently used language in North America. Second, the signs are standardized and easily recognized by signers across the United States. If children learn different signs at home, at daycare, and at church, then they will become confused and frustrated. This practice could also pose a safety risk. For example, if my toddler needs to stop immediately because of an oncoming car, I want him to recognize the sign STOP because it is used at home, the daycare center, the playground, church, and Grandma's house. Similarly, if my baby needs help, I want those around to understand very clearly what he needs. I have a story that illustrates just this point. One day, when Sean was a toddler, we were outside playing and gardening when the phone rang. In the moment it took me to retrieve the cordless phone from inside, Sean and our two very big dogs took off. We live on a dirt road on top of a hill that is surrounded by dense forest. Sean could have headed in any direction or even worse into the woods. I called one of our dear friends, who is also thankfully a neighbor and who knows some signs, and asked her to come help me with the frantic search. As Nancy was driving up the dirt road to our home she met quite an unlikely hiking team—Sean with a big walking stick in his hand and the two dogs, both of them much taller than Sean, were making their way down the hill. Sean looked at Nancy, smiled, and calmly signed HELP. If we are going to spend the time and energy to sign with our babies I strongly feel that using standardized ASL signs is the best and safest way to go.

3

A Time to Teach, A Time to Learn

Infants and toddlers learn differently than older children and adults. Planning a lesson and having an organized structured time for teaching signs is not realistic and is rarely productive. What actually works the best is very straightforward: simply start using signs as part of your child's daily routine. Everyday activities provide the perfect opportunity for teaching signs. It is as simple as using a basic sign during a frequently occurring activity; your child will begin to recognize the sign, associate it with a particular concept, and then will use it when she is ready.

Child development experts interpreted the research of ten, twenty, thirty years ago to mean that a child's memory did not develop until the sixth month of life and the cognitive ability to communicate did not exist before age two.[11] These milestones were readily accepted as fact and were taught as such for many years. However, anyone who actually works closely and spends time with very young children experiences a different reality. Those of us who have the pleasure of being in the presence of an infant are very aware that babies can begin to respond to familiarity. They recognize voices, smells, and the touch of familiar people, which indicates strongly that recall must begin developing much earlier than previously had been thought.

Recent studies on the cognitive abilities of newborns and infants and on when and how memory develops have yielded amazing results. According to Dr. Carolyn Rovee-Collier of Rutgers University, a baby's long-term memory can last up to twenty-four hours at six weeks of age. Although six-month-old infants do learn more rapidly and remember longer than infants half their age, their memory process follows the same basic pattern. Rovee-Collier suggests that developing routines for frequent activities and following the routines on a daily basis is a great exercise for infant memory development. This establishes predictability, comfort, and healthy expectations. It is easier for a child to remember a new skill that is experienced in many short sessions, rather than a few long playtimes. Rovee-Collier's work

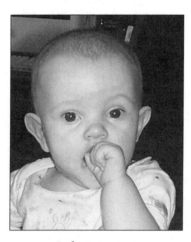

Infant signing
MILK/NURSE

Signing NURSE
to a newborn

shows that when eighteen minutes of total playtime with a repetitive activity is spread out over three days instead of one or two days, a baby can remember that skill for up to two weeks.[12]

I have been a parent for twenty-one years and a pediatric nurse and parent educator for twenty-five years. I have worked with thousands of families with small children over this time. My experience and personal study on the use and application of signing with hearing infants has provided both consistent and very exciting results. I have identified two essential milestones that indicate a child's readiness to learn signs. The first clue of sign readiness is a child's ability to initiate focused eye contact, even if only briefly. As early as four to six weeks of age, a baby will begin to watch a parent or loving caregiver's face as she speaks. At this stage, babies seem to be able distinguish between their dad and the lampshade, which is truly a heart-filled exciting time for parents. The second clue of sign readiness is marked by a baby's ability to intentionally smile in response to the environment. This typically can be expected at about two months of age. We all know that very young infants can and do smile much earlier than this, but we cannot know for sure what prompts the smile.

Gestures will begin to take on symbolic meaning when a child is able to demonstrate intentional gaze and is able to respond positively to the environment. These simple gestures or signs begin to represent specific things in the child's world. Keep in mind that a two-month-old has very basic interaction with the external world. His world revolves around the need for nourishment, warmth, safety, and a loving caregiver.

One of the true highlights of parenting is the recognition of the very unique connection between ourselves and our child. The moment that we understand the importance of mutual communication represents a wonderful learning opportunity for everyone. In this instant, parents experience an innocence that can only be taught by a child. The skills your baby learns at this moment are directly related to what he experiences from you. At this stage, it is very beneficial to begin demonstrating simple, one-hand signs. Parents who learn and model signing early tend to have babies who sign early. After all, deaf parents sign to their deaf and hearing babies from birth, and many begin to produce their first signs very early and by ten months of age can develop some fluency.[13]

Children will use whatever method is available as their desire to express themselves grows. They usually do not begin speaking in two- and three-word sentences until they

Toddler signing EAT

Infant signing CHANGE

are at least two years of age because it takes that long for the fine motor skills needed for vocalization to develop. However, visual and muscular coordination are in place long before this, so signing becomes an easy and natural method of expression.

Most children begin to engage in pretend play related to familiar activities by their first birthday. A one-year-old also typically exhibits the ability to choose between objects and to better understand the use of objects. Motor skills continue to develop as coordination improves and, by twenty-four months, a toddler's development allows for much more fluent sign and verbal abilities.

I strongly advise parents and caregivers of preverbal hearing children to use signs to augment their spoken words. This is particularly important in the early phases of learning sign. When we use sign to supplement our speech, the child hears the words, sees the gesture, and kinesthetically is able to experience the activity. The information received is reinforced by the different modalities and, therefore, the concept can be much more quickly and easily understood. For example, on your way to the changing area say something like "let's go change your diaper," and demonstrate the sign CHANGE to reinforce the concept.

Children will attach the meaning you intend to a sign if you use the sign in the correct situation. For instance, as the family dog barks and runs over to you, sign DOG and say "Here comes our doggie." The child will learn the concept in association with the gesture, the word, and the experience. One day, I was in our kitchen preparing for an upcoming signing conference. Sean, who had just turned two years old, wanted to help sort my overheads. I held up a still photo of Aleah at four months signing CHANGE and asked him what Aleah was saying. His response was clear—"Aleah is signing 'please change my diaper,' Mommy." Sean obviously understood not only Aleah's sign but also the concept she was expressing.

4

Getting Started

Starting out at a pace that is enjoyable and not overwhelming for parents is vitally important. If the adults are not having fun, how can we expect the babies to want to participate? When sign is used with a fun and relaxed attitude children will naturally want to take part. Enjoying the process is also beneficial in maintaining the commitment and dedication needed for success in signing with young children. It is essential that adults demonstrate the use of signs frequently and consistently because this directly influences a child's willingness to use sign.

Young children have a natural attraction to movement that combines wonderfully with their focus of attention, and parents can use this interest to foster the learning of signs. I suggest beginning with signs associated with the three Fs— family, food, and function. Most families find that the following signs are realistic and most appropriate to use in the very early phase of signing with their babies: MOMMY, DADDY, MILK, EAT, DRINK, CHANGE, and MORE. Almost all parents refer to themselves as *mommy* and *daddy* when talking to their infants, so begin to use the signs as soon as you begin talking to your baby.

MILK/NURSE

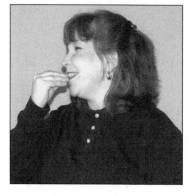

EAT

CHANGE

MORE

I have found that the best food sign to begin using with children under six months of age is MILK. This same sign can be used for NURSE and then later to indicate cow or soy milk for older children. Around six months of age, when a child begins taking solid food, parents can begin using the signs EAT and DRINK accordingly. The sign MORE is also helpful to help children express that they want more of whatever they

DRINK

MUSIC

Toddler signing FLOWER

Infant signing SNOW

already have— MORE to eat, MORE play, MORE music, etc. At this age, you can also begin to add the next F category—fun. Signs like MUSIC, FLOWER, and SNOW can be included in the early phases of play.

I suggest using CHANGE only in reference to diapers until the child is consistently using the toilet. By limiting the use of this specific sign we can avoid a lot of unnecessary confusion.

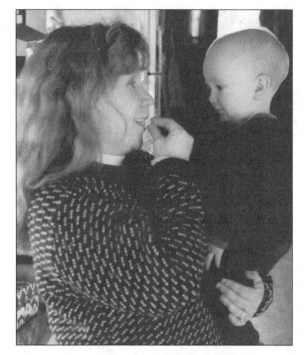

Demonstrating EAT to an infant

Parenting can be tough enough; do we really want to be won-dering "change what?" when it comes to dirty diapers?

Remember that signs are used to augment speech. Each time you say the word "eat," demonstrate the sign EAT. Do the same with MILK/NURSE (or formula), DRINK, MORE, and CHANGE. As discussed earlier it is essential that signs are demonstrated frequently and consistently along with the spoken word at the time of the associated behavior. This will result in the child learning the concept, sign, and spoken word. The child will be able to reproduce the sign long be-fore she has the fine motor coordination to say the word.

With practice, signing becomes more spontaneous and fluent for both the adults and children.

It is not realistic to expect hearing parents to learn ASL fluently in order to sign with their hearing babies. Because of its grammatical structure, ASL does not have a one-to-one correspondence with English. It is not possible to speak English and sign ASL at the same time. The stress of trying to sign and talk at the same time can subtract from the communication experience itself; it is not necessary for our purposes to sign each word in a spoken phrase. The spontaneity of conversations with children is priceless and can be lost in an instant. I suggest that we focus on the meaning, not the individual words. Choose signs for only the most significant words of the concept. Particularly in early signing, use one or two signs to convey an idea. Keeping the process easy can make all the difference in maintaining the level of commitment necessary for successful signing with babies. As time goes on, adding spoken and signed vocabulary occurs naturally.

Again, I encourage you to begin with the basics when signing with your hearing babies, even if you are fluent with ASL. A certain rhythm develops when signing with youngsters, and, as we will discuss in the next several chapters, there is much more to signing than just knowing the right sign.

5

Moments of Receptiveness

I have found that children absorb information much more easily in certain moments than in others. There are times that a child hungers for ways to convey needs, desires, and ideas. These moments of receptiveness can come and go in the blink of an eye, and their true potential is never really appreciated. But, when you are teaching signs to your baby, you must watch for and anticipate these moments of receptiveness when your child will have greater learning potential. In the moment of focused, direct eye contact, your baby's interest tends to be at a high point. This is also the moment most conducive to clear communication.

Getting a youngster's attention may be as easy as calling his name or touching her hand. If a child refuses to look your way, go ahead and sign anyway and have confidence in your child's peripheral vision. You will be quite surprised when out of the blue your baby will demonstrate that very sign in the near future.

Dr. Joseph Garcia describes three gazes to watch for when teaching signs to your baby. *Expressive gaze* refers to eye contact that occurs because the baby is in need of something. Offering a sign during that brief gaze seems to have a significant impact. For example, if you anticipate that your baby is getting hungry and is going to need to nurse or to have a bottle, be attentive and watch for the expressive gaze (you can usually see this immediately before a cry). In this moment of focused, direct eye contact sign MILK/NURSE as you say, "Do you want to nurse?" or "Let's get your bottle." Even at a very young age your baby will readily learn the sign MILK/NURSE and the concept of feeding. Your baby is literally hungry for a means to communicate his or her need.

The second type of gaze that signals high receptiveness is called *chance mutual gaze.* This occurs spontaneously when you and your child look at each other by chance. When that chance moment of focused, direct eye contact occurs, offer a sign for whatever you want to say—HELLO, I LOVE YOU, MOMMY, or BABY are several ideas.

Garcia describes the third type of gaze as *pointed gaze,* and it refers to focused eye contact made in response to something. For instance, when the screen door opens and daddy

I LOVE YOU

BABY

Demonstrating FATHER to an infant

walks in jingling his keys, your baby looks at daddy and then at you. In the moment that your baby looks at you, sign FATHER. This is another powerful opportunity for learning. Seize the moment!

In my years of working with parents and caregivers, I have discovered that natural instincts help us recognize other moments of high receptivity in our children. As parents, we attentively look into our baby's face and anxiously await the "moment of recognition." This is the instant when our babies recognize us as someone special. In this moment our heart flutters, we offer a smile, a tear of happiness, and soft loving words such as "I am your mommy" and offer the appropriate sign— MOTHER, FATHER, GRANDMOTHER, UNCLE.

As your children grow and their world becomes full, they will get into the habit of acquiring new signs. You will then begin to recognize what I call the "show me" look. Children who are accustomed to learning signs will turn to you inquisitively when they encounter a new object, person, or experience. They will demonstrate a "show me" look, fully expecting to learn a sign. If signing is new to you, I suggest keeping a reference guide in the diaper bag at all times during this phase of learning. One of my personal favorites is *Teach Your Tot to Sign* by Stacy Thompson and illustrated by Valerie Nelson-Metlay. This way you can take advantage of every opportunity to learn and teach new signs.

6

Practical Techniques and Helpful Hints

Researchers, early childhood educators, and parents have identified similar teaching strategies that can be very useful with all children, whether they are hearing, deaf, or have special needs. These basic and practical techniques for teaching signs to babies can be modified slightly and used successfully with older children, too.

Eye Contact

Once you make eye contact, the challenge is to maintain your child's attention. By using facial expressions, voice intonation, energy, and body posturing, you will have a huge influence on the attention span of your child. Your baby will observe your communication pattern and enthusiasm and then mimic it. If the adults in a child's life are excited about signing, the child will be excited too. It just happens that way with youngsters!

Hand Dominance

I am frequently asked "What hand should I use when I am signing?" or "What hand should my baby use?" The answer is both simple and complicated at the same time. In many two-hand signs, one hand moves or performs the action and the other hand is stationary and acts as a base. Older signers who have a hand preference should use their dominant hand as their action hand and their nondominant hand as their base hand. If you are right-handed, then your action hand would consistently be your right hand. If you are left-handed, then you will use your left hand. For little signers, right- versus left-hand dominance is not an issue, it simply does not matter. True hand dominance does not typically develop until a child nears school age. However, if a young child asks what hand to use, an appropriate response is "What hand do you want to use?" or "Which one feels more comfortable?"

Line of Sight

Imagine a line between your eyes and the eyes of your child. This area is referred to as the *line of sight*, and within this space you are able to maintain eye contact and your child can receive signs with uninterrupted focus. Parents can greatly enhance their child's ability to perceive specific movements by placing their signing/action hand in front of their face, just below the line of sight. When signs are displayed to the side (for example, at your shoulder area), young children tend to perceive them with much less focus or what I refer to as *peripheral focus*.

At one of the signing classes I held several years ago, a mother who is fluent in ASL asked me if I could help her interpret a specific gesture her two-year-old son frequently produced. He held his clenched fist at shoulder level and ever so slightly opened and closed his fist, making very small, fine, repetitive motions. I could not help but smile when I asked this mom to show me how she signs NO to her son. This sign is normally made by tapping the index and middle fingers on the thumb several times while placing the forearm at a 45-degree angle in front of the body. Done this way, the hand is at shoulder level, to the side of midline, and well below the line of sight. A child can only see a vague, fine motor movement, not the specific sign, which explains why the two-year-old made the sign as he did.

Repetition

The old saying "practice makes perfect" is true in signing with young children. Through repetition and modeling, the signs become imprinted into the child's memory. I find that signing everyday words each time they are spoken helps the process become habit. One of our goals is for our babies to develop their language skills so that communication naturally blossoms.

I recommend that parents sign, sign, sign. Each time you show a sign to your child, immediately repeat it and repeat it again. After demonstrating a specific sign several times, try to shape and mold your child's hands into making the sign. Some children are more comfortable with this technique of molding and shaping of their hands than others. If your efforts are met with resistance, simply try again at another time.

Imitation

Sign with other adults in your baby's presence. For example, when both parents are sitting at the dinner table, sign PLEASE, THANK YOU, MORE, and DRINK as appropriate. When adults, particularly parents, verbally communicate and use signs to augment their words, the child learns that signing is natural and acceptable. We know that even very young children love to imitate, and I have seen many babies emulate signs by watching their parents sign. Parents and teachers all over the country have experienced very similar situations. When they sign more, the babies sign more too.

Synonyms and Homonyms

American Sign Language frequently has one particular sign for several English words that have similar meanings

THANK YOU

PLEASE

(synonyms). For example one sign is used to mean *calm* and *quiet*; similarly the same sign is used for *bright* and *light*. When signing, think about the meaning of what you are trying to communicate. Synonyms like *toilet, potty,* and *go to the bathroom* (the noun and the verb) are all conveyed with the same sign.

BATHROOM/TOILET

FAMILY

The letters of the manual alphabet are often used to create a group or category of signs that have similar meanings. This is called *initialization*. For instance the sign GROUP can be changed to mean FAMILY or CLASS by using the G, F, and C handshapes respectively. This may seem confusing, but actually it makes learning much easier. By modifying one sign, many words can be clearly communicated.

ASL has different ways to express homonyms or words that look the same in English but have different meanings. For example, the sign RUN is signed differently in each of the following phrases: run around the playground, run a business, and have a runny nose. Occasionally, one single sign is used for multiple meanings. The sign ORANGE can mean either a type of fruit or a color. This form of signing homonyms occurs less frequently, but it does happen in some circumstances.

Nighttime Signing

When signing becomes more spontaneous, consistency of use also increases. You may find yourself or your child signing in dreams, or at least very capable of comfortably signing during those middle of the night awakenings. When you walk into a room to find a crying baby signing SCARED, you have tremendous insight on how to comfort that child. If the baby is signing DRINK or COLD, you know what to do. As the habit of signing brings a new level of fluency and more security, your child learns that her needs will be met even in times of stress.

For parents who are struggling with babies who want to sleep during the day and be awake at night, I offer a new twist on an old approach. When your baby awakens at night, do not speak, only whisper and sign. Keep lights off or very dim; this demonstrates that the noise level and atmosphere at night is markedly different from daytime. Babies will learn the difference between active daytime routines and nighttime ex-

DREAM

pectations. The value of clear communication is reinforced, and your baby's needs are met with less frustration.

Being in the Present Moment

It is very important to stay in the here and now when signing with your child. If you are fully in the present moment, you will be able to sign in the proper context, which will make your signs more meaningful. If you try to teach the sign for *cookie* when you are not making cookies or getting ready to eat a cookie, you could start a riot. As parents and teachers, we must take advantage of situations as they occur and unfold. If Grandma wants to see Sean sign BUTTERFLY, then Grandma and Sean will need to go outside or look in a book

A toddler signing BUTTERFLY
at a butterfly habitat

to find a butterfly. Remember, we are encouraging our babies to see, hear, and experience language as we facilitate learning at this moment.

Different Signs from Different Sources

Just as English has regional dialects, ASL has regional variations. For example, there are several different signs for *birthday* and *soda pop,* and the sign you use depends on what part of the country you reside in. All these regional signs are standard and accepted in their particular area. Most teachers suggest choosing the version used most consistently in your community. Also, choose the variation that offers the largest, simplest movement because it will be easier for infants and toddlers to make that sign.

MOTHER

FATHER

Incorporating Gender

Some signs include gender in their meaning, and they are made at a specific place on the face. The basic rule is that feminine nouns are signed along the jawline or on the chin, and masculine nouns are made at the temple or on the forehead. For example, both MOTHER and FATHER are made with a 5 handshape that taps on the face—on the chin for MOTHER and on the forehead for FATHER. Similarly, GIRL is signed on the jawline and BOY is signed on the forehead.

Signing in Public

I recommend that parents and caregivers sign in public exactly as they do at home. Using signs consistently, regardless of changing environments, is a powerful teaching tool because it provides a sense of constancy and reliability to your child. Signing for show or to entertain others in the early phases of learning sign is very confusing to your child and also detrimental to the intimate communication that you are working to build with your baby. A few years ago, a local television station wanted to interview me about using ASL with hearing infants and asked if they could film Sean signing. My response was candid; I told them I would gladly do the interview, but Sean (who was one year old) would decide at the time how he would participate. As it turned out, Sean loved the reporter. She was very bright and she brought popcorn and bubbles to jump start the bonding process. Everyone had a great time—we laughed, we played, and we signed— and that day it just happened to be caught on film.

7

Visual Capabilities of Young Children

Vision is usually a newborn's most underdeveloped sense. Your baby's eyes actually change and mature in shape during early childhood, and these changes directly affect your youngster's visual acuity. The visual haze present at birth gradually disappears, and, by two months of age, a baby is able to fixate on moving objects. The ability to focus develops over the first several months of life. In these early months, there seems to be what I refer to as a visual sweet spot between eight and twelve inches from a baby's face. At this distance, your baby's eyes accommodate and make clear vision possible in short intervals. Between four and six months of age, eye-hand coordination develops and babies begin to prefer more complex visual stimuli. Depth perception begins to develop by seven to nine months but may actually exist earlier as an innate safety mechanism.

Infants do have visual preferences. In early infancy they react more to bright or contrasting moving objects. Human babies seem to readily develop a preference for looking at the human face. As early as six to eight weeks of age, babies typically begin to respond to human faces more than inanimate objects. By two to three months, infants seem to be able to

Demonstrating the sign
MOTHER

recognize familiar individuals and familiar objects like a feeding bottle. By six months, infants have the visual focus to distinguish facial expressions and can also differentiate between familiar and strange faces.[14]

When signing to babies younger than six months of age, it is important to maintain eye contact and proximity. Keep your signs within the baby's field of vision, which is typically eight to twelve inches from your baby's face. One-hand signs are the most feasible to use with very young babies. Signs like MILK/NURSE, MOTHER, and FATHER are particularly easy to do and are most appropriate at this stage of life. What could possibly be more important?

Babies older than six months typically have a more expanded field of vision. The ability to see at a peripheral range of 180 degrees and to a distance of several feet brings many new objects into view. Signing at a distance gradually becomes possible. I suggest taking cues from your baby to note his ability to maintain attention, exhibit a receptive gaze, and to respond to signs. You can expect your child's vision to increase by one to one-and-a-half feet per month for the first year of life. Babies are great at letting us know when we need to do something different, like repositioning, so pay attention to how your baby responds at various distances. Small children simply look away when their focus and interest shifts. I have found that the best gauges of a baby's visual capabilities are his ability to maintain eye contact and to focus attention on a person or an object.

8

Waiting for Baby's First Sign

Some folks describe the anticipation of their baby's first sign as similar to the excitement associated with childbirth. We never can be sure when a baby will start producing signs. My best advice for "expectant" parents and caregivers is to be patient, enjoy the process, and keep signing. One day when you least expect it, your baby will naturally and calmly start signing. Usually a baby's first sign will be one of the basic food/family/function-related signs that you have been using. Hold on because after that first sign, the second and third will be close behind.

There are several things you can do to motivate a child to start producing signs. Gently tapping your child's hand when you want a gestured response reminds her that you are expecting and waiting for a sign. Another very effective technique is to actually demonstrate signs on your child's hand. This technique reinforces the concept of hearing, seeing, and experiencing the concept.

Those of us who are accustomed to being around little ones know that sometimes we need to be very creative to take advantage of an opportunity. When you notice your baby's attention is focused on something in the environment (other

An older infant signing DRINK, then receiving a drink

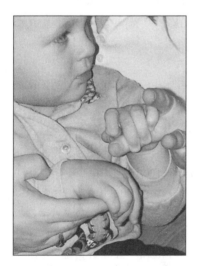 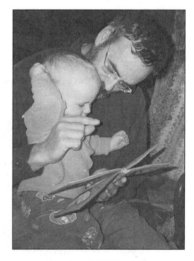

Demonstrating GENTLE on
the hands of a child

Signing BIRD while
reading

than you), seize the moment to teach a new sign. For instance, if your baby is completely mesmerized by a bird outside your window, get between your baby and the window and demonstrate the sign BIRD. This technique also reinforces the concept of signing in proper context; your baby learns as she is appreciating the moment.

Many parents and childcare providers take great pride in the ability to anticipate the needs of their youngsters. After all, if we are a step ahead, conflicts can be resolved before they occur, whining can be minimized, and most meltdowns can be avoided. These are very good reasons to stay ahead of the troops, but I suggest that we also consider the benefit of briefly delaying our response to our child's request. Allowing a short pause between your child's demand and your response may indeed give your baby the opportunity to sign what it is she wants. The following scenario illustrates this technique.

> While sitting at the table for a meal, you anticipate that your child will want a drink very soon. Instead of placing a cup within your child's reach before he wants a drink, place the cup at a distance that requires him to ask for it. You can then tap your baby's hand to remind him to sign. This delay should only be ten seconds or so; more than that probably would result in a less than enjoyable meal. I have found that, as parents, we must choose our battles wisely; tears, yelling, and chaos over signing (or dinner) is not productive.

The day will come when the baby in your life quite naturally will begin to convey specific needs or wants through sign. This is a time to celebrate and show your enthusiasm! Acknowledge the sign and immediately reward your child.

After those first attempts at signing are rewarded with the object of desire, your child will be motivated to use more signs. If your baby girl signs EAT, reward her with a treat that she enjoys. She will learn that her signing results in her needs being readily met. This will reinforce learning, security, and the benefits of signing.

Adding Vocabulary

After your baby begins using his or her first signs, more signs will gradually come. Over the next few weeks or months your baby will develop a core group of five to ten signs. He will use these signs daily to convey routine thoughts and needs. Parents, caregivers, and educators of young children should consider the time that children are using only their core group of signs as a grace period. The core group of signs enables babies to become comfortable and secure in the process of signing. And while they are watching the adults in their world, their receptive vocabulary increases. During this time, I recommend that adults actively build their signing vocabulary. Do not limit yourselves to only the signs your baby can demonstrate. At this stage of learning, babies need signs, signs, and more signs.

As young children learn to sign, the signs become more frequently used, more spontaneous, and more natural. Once children are comfortable with this core group of signs, there then tends to be an explosion of sign. Learning becomes much easier because children absorb and can produce a cornucopia of signs. At this point in time the only limit to what your child will sign is what you will be able to teach. This is usually the time you will see your baby's "show me" look. This specific focused-direct eye contact that is initiated by your child lets you know that the child is expecting to learn a new sign from you! Your young child will look directly into your eyes and wait for you to show her the appropriate sign relating to the new situation or object.

At this point, many parents begin to carry a sign book so they can find the right sign at the right time. The quality of illustrations and explanation are easier to interpret in some manuals than in others. Some have easily understood written directions for each sign, and some have no directions at all. Dictionaries can be directed to a certain market or population and are usually alphabetized. Other references tend to use categories or groups of related signs. You can also find several virtual signing dictionaries available online. I have already mentioned that Stacy Thompson's *Teach Your Tot to Sign* is one of my favorite resources; you can find more sign books in the selected references section.

9

Interpreting the Signs of Babies

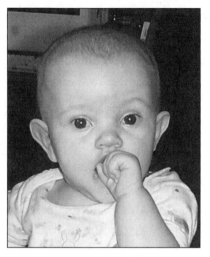

Infant signing MILK/NURSE

Infants develop motor skills gradually, so it is important to know what to expect at different ages. Early signs can be easily missed, so you must watch closely. If you notice that your baby is making an odd or different type of movement, think out of the box— it could be a sign! Young children will actually practice making a sign, and, if we are perceptive, we can watch the crude movement evolve into a recognizable sign. For example, grasping occurs during the first two to three months as a reflex and over time it becomes voluntary.

A four-month-old baby may try to sign MILK/NURSE, but it can look like an awkward waving motion with a closed fist. By seven to nine months, a much more precise MILK/NURSE gesture is clearly evident and very easily identified.

Recognizing that a child is attempting a sign can be tricky, and understanding the sign can also be a big challenge. Young children can only approximate the handshapes of many intended signs. They produce an *approximation,* in other words, an immature version of a sign that resembles but is not exactly like the standard version. For example when young children first sign MORE, they usually produce an approximation. The formal version of MORE is made by tapping the fingertips of both hands together several times. Approximations of MORE can look like two fists coming together or even two open hands brought together. Many times the sign will evolve to an index finger on one hand touching the open palm of the other. This form of immature signing is

Approximations of MORE

Formal MORE

similar to a verbal approximation, like when a toddler says "wawa" instead of "water."

In addition to making approximations, babies also over-generalize the meaning of a sign while they explore its appro-priate use. Many children use their first signs for everything they want to communicate. For example, if a child's first sign is MILK/NURSE, his initial interpretation may be that he gets whatever he wants when he opens and closes his fist. Keep in mind that children under six months of age have very basic needs and their only desire may be to nurse or have a bottle.

Another sign that is frequently overgeneralized is MORE. Instead of first signing what they want, children may simply sign MORE. If your baby means he wants to eat but signs something else, I have found that it is most productive to acknowledge the attempt and clarify the meaning by showing the correct sign. With repetition your baby's sign will become more like yours.

Sometimes, though, we forget that children see life from a different perspective. We can make the assumption that a baby is using the wrong sign, but in fact we can be the ones who are mistaken. I have a great example from when my son Sean was about a year old. One afternoon in his room, he kept signing BIRD. I did not see a bird, so I assumed he was confusing this sign with another. Later I saw the Nike swoosh on a gym bag next to his crib, and I realized that Sean was right; it did look like a bird.

Many signs look alike in the early days of infant signing. The waving open hand of a young child can be the sign for *father, cow, airplane,* or *I love you.* In the attempt to interpret the meaning of your child's sign, first check the location of the sign—is the hand held high or low? Next look at the type of handshape—is the hand opened or closed? Then look at

Is it DADDY, COW, AIRPLANE,
or I LOVE YOU?

the movement—is it small or large? Next take a look at the overall situation—are you inside or outside? What do you see or hear that your baby can also observe? Finally, take a really good guess. If you are outside and the baby looks up because she hears an airplane or helicopter, that may be what she is trying to share with you. The most important response is to be positive. Even if your guess is not quite right, your baby will know that you are paying attention and that you are excited about her attempts at signing. Keep guessing; if at first you don't succeed try, try again. It may also be helpful to ask someone who knows ASL.

Parents, therapists, and caregivers frequently ask me to interpret a child's sign. The sign in question is usually repeated frequently by the child. He tends to use the sign consistently, but it makes no sense at all to the grown ups. When this test-the-teacher opportunity arises, I try to think out of the box of adult perceptions by asking several important questions.

1. What is the situation that prompts the child to use the sign?
2. How does the child seem to be feeling when the sign is made? Does he look happy, excited, or like he needs something urgently? Or is he signing in a matter-of-fact way?
3. When does the child stop using the sign?
4. Can the adult mimic the child's sign?

Once I have the answers to these questions, I step back and try to see the situation through the child's eyes. I also try to imagine the child's feelings in the particular situation. Then, I consider that the sign in question most likely will relate to one of the four Fs (family, food, function, and fun). Lastly, I take a really good guess. Usually, I can figure out what the child is signing; after adults catch on to this process, they can also decipher the child's signs.

During an Adult Continuing Education class I recently taught, the mother of a five-month-old baby girl raised her hand and said, "There is a motion my daughter has just started making and I don't know what it is." She explained that the baby uses the sign when her daddy is near or when people are talking about him (the father, who is in the Coast Guard, had just gone back to sea). This young mother stated that her baby usually seemed excited and happy when she made the sign. The mom demonstrated the gesture by taking her closed fist and tapping her forehead several times. I could not help but smile as I immediately knew the child was signing DADDY.

Deciphering early signs can be a big challenge at times, but eventually the signs will make perfect sense to both you and your baby. As you interpret a child's sign approximations, enthusiastically acknowledge the attempts and simply demonstrate the correct sign. This is called *modeling*. Children will want to continue their signing attempts and improve in their abilities when they receive positive reinforcement. By appreciating all attempts at signing and then modeling the correct sign, we praise our children and also clarify for them what is expected. As children's coordination and dexterity improve, so will their ability to produce formal signs.

10

What If I Do Not Know a Sign?

We all experience the frustration of wanting to sign something and either forgetting or not knowing the sign. Novice signers cling to their reference books and fluent signers always know where to find a good sign dictionary. You may find it helpful to have an American Sign Language dictionary so that you can find a sign when you need it. Keep in mind that ASL is different from English; you will not find a sign for every word in the English dictionary.

American Sign Language, like spoken language, continues to evolve. Over the thirty-five years that I have signed, I have seen many changes in ASL. Many signs that in the past were made strictly with two hands (for example, COW) now can be made with one or two hands. The base form of some signs has been modified so the sign is made with a different handshape that helps to clarify the meaning. This is called *initialization*, which I mentioned earlier. Another change that has occurred is the adoption of signs from other countries for their country names. Today, many ASL signers use the Australian sign for *Australia,* the German sign for *Germany,* the Spanish sign for *Spain,* etc., rather than the older ASL signs.

Standardized vocabulary continues to expand as well. A good ASL sign book thirty years ago had 500 signs; today's comprehensive references contain 2000–3000 sign illustrations. You can find signing resources in print, on DVDs, and online. Many high schools and colleges now offer American Sign Language as part of their language programs.

When you do not know the sign for an object or a concept, the first step is to check your favorite reference source. When you go on a walk in the park with your signing baby, you may want to take a pocket dictionary along. Trust me, you will use it! I strongly encourage the use of ASL signs whenever possible. After all, we want our children to understand and be understood by other signers. Families with deaf or hard of hearing children whose primary language is ASL need to keep strictly to ASL. However, some proponents of using signs with young children have introduced gestures that require less motor skill and are easier to produce. One

Formal HELP   Alternate HELP

example is the alternative sign for *help,* which was first published and endorsed by Joseph Garcia. This alternative gesture is signed with open hands repeatedly patting the upper chest with urgency.

All babies, even deaf babies, will create their own home-made signs naturally. Parents can choose to keep the home-spun sign or change it to ASL by modeling the standard sign. Be selective in the homemade signs that you and your baby use. It would probably be safe to make up a sign for *baboon,* but not acceptable to make up a sign for *hot.*

11

Some Final Thoughts

Signing offers our children a visual and physical way of learning concepts and language. When we use signs to augment our words, we offer our babies repeated language input visually, audibly, and physically. Babies who learn to sign their needs, wants, and ideas demonstrate increased self-esteem and are empowered to interact in their world with much more clarity. Signing with your baby also promotes early language and literacy skills.

We all learn by repetition, so repeat a sign every time you demonstrate it to your child. Repeat, repeat, repeat is a great rule to follow. In the early stages of learning, offer a specific sign before, during, and after the activity associated with that sign. Children will learn the intended meaning of a sign when it is shown in proper context and repeated consistently and frequently. Signing as part of a child's daily routine seems to be one of the most effective ways of teaching and building recall. Signing stories and songs can be fun and interesting for everyone in the family.

Signing enhances the parent–child bonds and enriches adult–child interactions. Closer relationships can develop because of this two-way communication. This very early and effective method of relating to babies promotes a new age of parenting. Parents and caregivers are able to develop clear and natural communication patterns with their infants and toddlers.

Eventually your child will enthusiastically use signs for most of her needs. When your baby wants milk, she will sign MILK. When she needs help, she will produce the sign before the frustration sets in. While we want to reinforce early signing by responding to our children's requests, there will be a time when we need to set boundaries. Older signers have an important lesson to learn, which is: just because they can sign what they want does not necessarily mean they will always get what they sign.

Once your baby knows the sign for a particular thing, it is perfectly reasonable and necessary to set limits. Children naturally test limits to learn where the limits are. Some of the signs that naturally express limits are SHARE, STOP, GENTLE, and WAIT.

Let me describe two different scenarios. Suppose that ten minutes before dinner is ready your fifteenth-month-old signs COOKIE. What do you do? Well, if your toddler has been signing for a while and has a large signing vocabulary, this may be the time to consider saying, "I see you signed cookie, that's wonderful! We need to wait for a cookie. Let's get a book now." Then, sign WAIT or NO, COOKIE, and BOOK. However, if this is one of your fifteenth-month-old's first signs or is a brand new sign for him, you need a different response. Get a cookie and celebrate and then have dinner.

I have a story that illustrates the wonderful benefits of signing. One evening several years ago, I received a phone

NO

COOKIE

BOOK

call from a very excited grandfather whose signing fifteen-month-old grandson had just come for a visit. Earlier that day, grandma and grandson went to the Maine Blueberry Festival, which is an old-fashioned country fair with livestock, 4-H competitions, pie contests, and such. As this unsuspecting grandfather tucked his grandbaby in bed, the child began signing excitedly. This otherwise preverbal young child started signing to his grandfather all of the wonderful things he experienced during his day like PIG, COW, BALLOON, SLIDE, HORSE, CAR, BIRDS, GOAT, TRACTOR, and of course ICE CREAM. Granddad was so moved that he called me and said "Leann, it should be illegal not to teach babies to sign!" Just think, in the future this may be a first amendment issue—the right to communication for our babies.

Most children can learn to use signs readily while their vocal skills develop. As a child's verbal abilities increase, signing becomes less needed and less used. In some environments, such as classrooms or families with deaf or hard of hearing members, it is necessary to continue to use ASL. Children who outgrow signing seem to find ASL very easy to relearn when they take it as a language class in high school or college. In my experience, school-age children who signed as babies tend to have an affinity for fine motor activities, a love for books and literature, and confidence in their ability to explore life.

If you are a seasoned parent, childcare provider, or early childhood educator, your first adventures in signing will open several unexpected doors. First, do not be surprised if the quantity and duration of tantrums decreases as older infants and young toddlers begin signing. I have spoken with many parents who notice an immediate reduction in tantrums by their signing children. Some parents find themselves asking, "Doesn't my child need to have at least an occasional meltdown?" My answer is short and sweet—no! Children do not need to have tantrums. Tantrums do not seem to be developmentally essential. Giving your child more ability to communicate reduces the frustration levels that often cause tantrums.

Parents of signing babies usually find it beneficial to brush up on their observation skills. One beautiful summer day Sean and I headed to the lake. I was driving and he was sitting in his car seat behind me. To my dismay, Sean had been signing the entire trip and I missed it. I was so disappointed. I soon became an expert at strategically placing mirrors so that this would not happen again.

While on this journey of parenting, I ask you to remember to be loving, patient, and steadfast. Most of all, do not forget to have fun! Children learn through play, and offering your hearing infants and toddlers the opportunity to use ASL may be the very best thing for everyone. Give your baby a hug for me, sign, and have fun!

NOTES

The following articles and books have been mentioned in this text.

1. Jeff Grabmeier, "Infants Use Sign Language to Communicate at OSU Experimental School," *OSU Research News Service*, January 25, 1999, http://host.uniroma3.it/docenti/boylan/COURSES/gen/asl-kids.htm (accessed August 26, 2008).

2. Linda P. Acredolo and Susan Goodwyn, "The Long-Term Impact of Symbolic Gesturing during Infancy on IQ at Age 8" (paper presented at the meeting of the International Society for Infant Studies, Brighton, UK, July 2000).

3. Brie Moore, Linda Acredolo, and Susan Goodwyn, "Symbolic Gesturing and Joint Attention: Partners in Facilitating Verbal Development" (paper presented at the biennial meeting of the Society for Research in Child Development, Minneapolis, MN, April 2001).

4. Acredolo and Goodwyn, "Long-Term Impact."

5. Marilyn Daniels, "The Effects of Sign Language on Hearing Children's Language Development," *Communication Education* 43 (1994): 291–298; Daniels, "Seeing Language: The Effect over Time of Sign Language on Vocabulary Development in Early Childhood Education," *Child Study Journal* 26 (1996): 193–208.

6. Grabmieir, "Infants Use Sign Language."

7. Joseph Garcia, *Sign with Your Baby* (Seattle: Northlight Communications, 2003).

8. Sharon Gretz, "Using Sign Language with Children Who Have Apraxia of Speech," http://www.apraxia-kids.org /site /c.chKMI0PIIsE/b.980831/apps/s/content.asp?ct=464165; Claire Donovan, "Teaching Sign Language," *Disability Solutions* 2, no. 5 (1998): 1, 3–8; Larry D. Sensenig, Edward J. Mazeika, and Bridget Topf, "Sign Language Facilitation of Reading with Students Classified as Trainable Mentally Handicapped," *Education and Training in Mental Retardation* 24 (1989): 121–125.

9. Donna L. Wong, *Whaley & Wong's Essentials of Pediatric Nursing*, 5th ed. (St. Louis: Mosby, 1997).

10. Garcia, *Sign with Your Baby*.

11. Jean Piaget, *The Origins of Intelligence in Children*, trans. Margaret Cook (New York: International Universities Press, 1954).

12. Carolyn Rovee-Collier, "The Development of Infant Memory." *Current Directions in Psychological Science* 8 (1999): 81–85.

13. Karen Emmorey, *Language, Cognition, and the Brain: Insights from Sign Language Research* (Mahwah, NJ: Lawrence Erlbaum Associates, 2002), 172.

14. Wong, *Whaley & Wong's Essentials of Pediatric Nursing*.

SELECTED REFERENCES

Acredolo, Linda, and Susan Goodwyn. *Baby Signs*. New York: McGraw-Hill, 2002.

American Sign Language Browser. Communication Technology Laboratory, Michigan State University, 2000. http://commtechlab. msu.edu/sites/aslweb/browser.htm

Boyatzis, Chris J. "Gesture and Development: An Introduction to the Special Issue." *Journal of Nonverbal Behavior* 24, no. 2 (2000): 59–62.

Brown, Christopher. *The Art of Sign Language*. San Diego: Thunder Bay Press, 2002.

Brown, Roger. *A First Language: The Early Stages*. Cambridge, MA: Harvard University Press, 1973.

Daniels, Marilyn. *Dancing with Words: Signing for Hearing Children's Literacy*. Westport, CT: Bergin & Garvey, 2001.

Flodin, Mickey. *Signing for Kids*. Rev. ed. New York: Perigee Books, 2007.

———. *Signing Illustrated*. Rev. ed. New York: Perigee Books, 2004.

Goodwyn, Susan W., Linda P. Acredolo, and Catherine A. Brown. "Impact of Symbolic Gesturing on Early Language Development." *Journal of Nonverbal Behavior* 24, no. 2 (2000): 81–103.

Griffith, Penny L. "Mode-Switching and Mode-Finding in a Hearing Child of Deaf Parents." *Sign Language Studies* 48 (1985): 195–222.

Hall, S. S., and K. S. Weatherly. "Using Sign Language with Tracheotomized Infants and Toddlers." *Pediatric Nurse* 15, no. 4 (1989): 362–67.

Humphries, Tom, Carol Padden, and Terrence J. O'Rourke. *A Basic Course in American Sign Language.* 2nd ed. Silver Spring, MD: T. J. Publishers, 1994.

Moore, Timothy E., ed. *Cognitive Development and the Acquisition of Language.* New York: Academic Press, 1973.

Piaget, Jean. *Origins of Intelligence in Children.* Translated by Margaret Cook. New York: International Universities Press, 1952.

Riekehof, Lottie L. *The Joy of Signing: The Illustrated Guide for Mastering Sign Language and the Manual Alphabet.* 2nd ed. Springfield, MO: Gospel Publishing House, 1987.

Rovee-Collier, Carolyn. "Dissociation in Infant Memory: Rethinking the Development of Implicit and Explicit Memory." *Psychology Review* 104 (1997): 467–98.

Shapiro, Lawrence E. *The Secret Language of Children.* Naperville, IL: Sourcebook Inc., 2003.

Thompson, Stacy A. *Teach Your Tot to Sign: The Parents' Guide to American Sign Language.* Washington, DC: Gallaudet University Press, 2005.

GLOSSARY OF CHILD- AND FAMILY-ORIENTED SIGNS

AMERICAN MANUAL ALPHABET

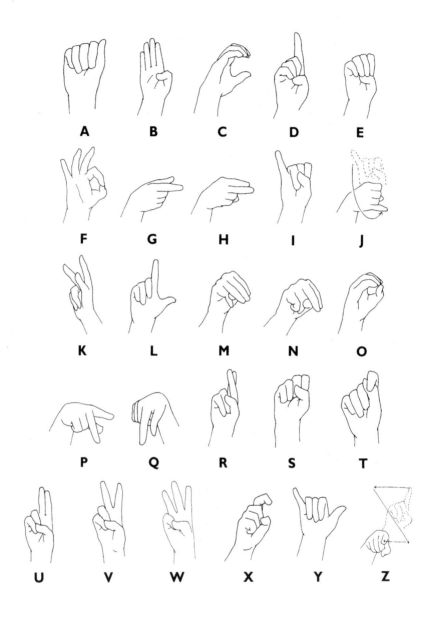

AIRPLANE
Move your hand forward in two quick motions.

APPLE
Twist the knuckle of your index finger on your cheek.

BABY

Place one hand inside the other and rock your arms back and forth as if cradling a baby.

BALL

Tap your fingertips together to form a ball.

BANANA
Move your right thumb and index finger tips down
your left index finger as if peeling a banana.

BATH
Rub your hands up and down your chest as if washing.

BEAR

Cross your wrists and scratch your fingers off your chest several times.

BEAUTIFUL/PRETTY

Move your open hand across your face and close your fingers.

BED
Rest your head on an open hand.

BEE
Flick your index finger against your cheek, then
quickly pat your cheek as if swatting a bee.

BICYCLE

Circle your hands forward in alternating motions as if pedaling a bicycle.

BIRD

Open and close your index finger and thumb in front of your mouth.

BIRTHDAY (1)

Put your middle finger on your chin and then move it down to your chest.

BIRTHDAY (2)

Tug on your ear lobe several times.

BLANKET
Move your hands up from your stomach to your
shoulders as if covering yourself with a blanket.

BOAT
Bounce your hands forward like a boat bouncing on
the waves.

BOOK

Press your hands together and then open them as if opening a book.

BOY

Tap your fingertips together two times.

BROTHER

Sign BOY and then bring your hand down until your index fingers touch.

BUBBLES

Flutter your fingers gently while your hands move up like bubbles floating in the air.

BUTTERFLY

Cross your thumbs and flutter your fingers like
butterfly wings as your hands move forward.

CANDY (1)

Twist your index finger on your cheek.

CANDY (2)
Brush your index and middle fingers down your chin
twice.

CAR
Move your hands up and down in a steering motion.

CAREFUL

Place one hand on top of the other and circle them around.

CAT

Brush your thumb and index finger tips off your cheek as if stroking whiskers.

CHANGE

Place your right hand on top of your left hand, then
rotate your hands until your left hand is on top.

CLEAN

Slide your right hand across your left palm.

COLD
Shake your fists as if your are shivering.

COME
Move your hands toward your chest in alternating circles.

COOKIE
Twist and bounce your right hand on your left palm.

COW
Place your thumbs on your temples and twist your
hands back and forth several times.

CRACKER

Gently tap your elbow several times.

CUP/BOTTLE

Place your right hand on your left palm as if holding a cup or bottle.

DANCE

Swing your index and middle fingers above your open palm.

DIRTY

Place your hand under your chin and wiggle your fingers.

DOCTOR

Tap your fingertips on the inside of your wrist as if checking your pulse.

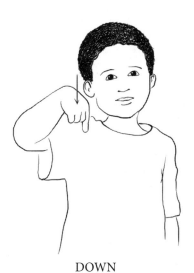

DOWN

Point your index finger down.

DRINK

Place your thumb at the side of your mouth and twist
your hand up.

DUCK

Open and close your hand in front of your mouth like
a duck's bill.

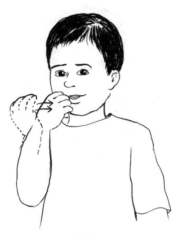

EAT

Tap your fingertips on your lips as if placing food in your mouth.

FALL DOWN

Stand your index and middle fingers on your open palm, then flip your hand over and land on your palm.

FAMILY

With your palms facing out, swing your hands around
in a circle until your little fingers touch.

FAST/QUICK

Point both index fingers straight out, then snap them
back very quickly.

FATHER

Place your thumb on your forehead and wiggle your fingers.

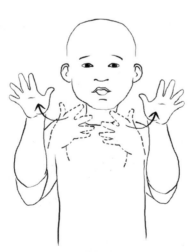

FINISH

Start with your palms facing toward you and quickly flip your hands around.

FISH

Wiggle your hand forward like a fish swimming in water.

FLOWER

Move your fingertips from one side of your nose to the other.

FULL
Move your hand up until it hits your chin.

FUNNY
Slide your index and middle fingers off your nose twice.

GET
Start with both hands open, then bring them toward
you while closing them as if grabbing something.

GIRL
Gently stroke your cheek with your thumb two times.

GOOD

Place your right fingertips on your chin, then bring
your hand down until it lands in your left palm.

GRANDFATHER

Start with your thumb on your forehead and bounce
your hand forward in two steps (indicating two
generations).

GRANDMOTHER
Start with your thumb on your chin and bounce your
hand forward in two steps (indicating two generations).

HAPPY
Brush your hands up off your chest several times.

HEAVY

Drop your hands down twice.

HELICOPTER

Place your right hand on your left thumb and rock
your hand side to side like the blades of a helicopter.

HELLO

Place your hand near your forehead and move it forward.

HELP

Put your right hand on your left palm and push your right hand up as if helping someone get up.

HOME

Place your fingertips near your chin and then arc your
hand up to your cheek.

HOT

Start with your fingertips near your mouth and then
quickly twist your hand around.

HURT/PAIN

Tap your index fingertips together over the area of the
body that hurts.

I LOVE YOU

Extend your thumb, index, and little finger and shake
your hand lightly.

JUMP

Bounce your index and middle fingers on your left palm several times.

KETCHUP

Tap the side of your left fist several times as if you are tapping the bottom of a ketchup bottle.

KISS

Gently tap the fingertips of both hands together and
then separate them.

LIGHT/BRIGHT

Hold your hands together with fingers touching and
then move your hands apart while opening them.

LIGHT (weight)

Place your hands, with palms facing out, in front of your chest, and then twist your hands around.

LIGHTNING

Swing your index finger down as if drawing a lightning bolt.

LISTEN

Place your hand against the back of your ear and tilt
your head slightly.

LITTLE/SHORT

Move your hand down in a bouncing motion to show
something getting shorter or smaller.

LOUD/THUNDER

Touch your ear with your index finger and then shake both hands back and forth firmly.

LOVE

Cross your hands on your chest and hunch your shoulders as if hugging yourself.

MEDICINE
Rock your middle finger on your palm as if crushing a pill.

MILK/NURSE
Open and close your fist several times as if milking a cow.

MONKEY
Scratch both sides of your trunk with an upward
motion, like a monkey.

MORE
Tap your fingertips together several times.

MOTHER

Place your thumb on your chin and wiggle your fingers.

MOTORCYCLE

Twist both hands up and down at the wrist as if revving a motorcycle.

MUSIC
Swing your right hand back and forth several times
inside your left arm as if conducting an orchestra.

MY/MINE
Pat your chest once for MY, twice for MINE.

NO

Tap your index and middle fingers on your thumb several times.

NOISY

Touch your ear with your index finger and then shake both hands back and forth.

NURSE

Tap the tips of your index and middle fingers on the inside of your wrist.

PACIFIER

Bring your fingers up to your mouth as if inserting a pacifier.

PASTA/SPAGHETTI

Place your little fingers together and then move your hands apart with a spiraling motion.

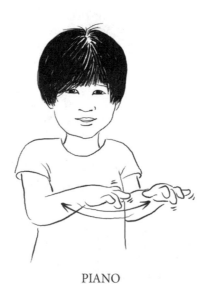

PIANO

Wiggle your fingers while moving your hands back and forth as if playing a keyboard.

PIG

Place the back of your hand under your chin and bend
your fingers several times.

PIZZA

Twist both hands up and down two times.

PLAY
Twist your hands back and forth several times.

PLEASE
Move your hand in a small circle on your chest.

RAIN

Start with your hands at shoulder level, then bounce your hands down in quick, short movements, like a rain shower.

SAD

Move your hands down in front of your face slowly like tears falling.

SAME

Bring your index fingers together and tap twice.

SAND

Rub your fingertips against your thumbs as you move your hands back and forth, as if dropping grains of sand.

SANDWICH

Bring your hands up to your mouth as if eating a sandwich.

SHARE

Swing your right hand side-to-side along your left index finger.

SHOES

Tap your fists together several times.

SISTER

Sign GIRL and then bring your hand down until your index fingers touch.

SIT

Move your right index and middle fingers down onto
your left index and middle fingers.

SLEEP

Move your open hand down your face slowly then
bring your fingertips together and close your eyes.

SLIDE

Slide your right hand down and away from your left hand as if going down a playground slide.

SLOW

Move your right hand slowly from the fingertips to the wrist of your left hand.

SNAKE

Start with your right hand near your nose, then move
your hand forward in a zigzag motion like a snake
slithering on the ground.

SNOW

Wiggle your fingers as your hands move slowly
downward like snow lightly falling.

SOCKS
Slide your index fingers back and forth.

SORRY
Move your hand in small circles on your chest.

SPIDER

Cross your hands and wiggle your fingers like spider legs crawling.

STAR

Slide your index fingers against each other as your hands move upward.

STOP

Firmly bring the side of your right hand down onto your left palm.

SWIM

Move your hands forward and out several times as if swimming the breast stroke.

TEACHER

Move your hands out from your forehead (the sign for *teach*) and then open your hands and move them straight down (the sign for *person*).

TELEPHONE

Hold your hand against the side of your face as if holding a telephone receiver.

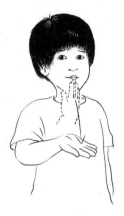

THANK YOU

Start with your fingers on your chin and then move your hand down.

TIRED

Start with your fingertips on your chest and then let your hands fall down on your chest as if you are exhausted.

TOILET/POTTY/BATHROOM
Shake your hand from side to side in small movements.

TOUCH
Gently tap the back of your left hand with your right
middle finger.

TRAIN

Slide your right index and middle fingers along your left index and middle fingers like a train moving on railroad tracks.

TRUCK

Move your right hand back from your left hand toward your shoulder.

UP

Point your index finger straight up.

WAIT

Angle your arms, with your left hand out a little
farther than your right hand, and wiggle your fingers.

WANT
Start with your arms extended and pull your hands in
toward your body while bending your fingers.

WATER
Tap your chin several times with your index finger.

WHERE

Wave your index finger from side to side.

WORK

Tap the heel of your right hand on the back of your left hand several times.

YES

Bend your wrist up and down several times as if nodding yes.